Facts About Countries
India

Lizann Flatt

SEA-TO-SEA

Mankato Collingwood London

This edition first published in 2009 by
Sea-to-Sea Publications
Distributed by Black Rabbit Books
P.O. Box 3263
Mankato, Minnesota 56002

Printed in China

Library of Congress Cataloging-in-Publication Data:

Flatt, Lizann.
  India / Lizann Flatt.
    p. cm. -- (Facts about countries)
  Includes index.
  Summary: "Describes the geography, history, industries,
education, government, and cultures of India. Includes maps,
charts, and graphs"--Provided by publisher.
  ISBN 978-1-59771-117-3
  1. India--Juvenile literature. I. Title.
  DS407.F563 2009
  954--dc22
                              2008004636

9 8 7 6 5 4 3 2

Published by arrangement with the Watts Publishing
Group Ltd, London.

Facts About Countries is produced for Franklin
Watts by Bender Richardson White, PO Box 266,
Uxbridge, UK.

Editors: Lionel Bender, Angela Royston
Designer and Page Make-up: Ben White
Picture Researcher: Cathy Stastny
Cover Make-up: Mike Pilley, Radius
Production: Kim Richardson

Graphics and Maps: Stefan Chabluk
Educational Advisor: Prue Goodwin, Institute of
Education, The University of Reading
Consultant: Dr. Terry Jennings, a former geography
teacher and university lecturer. He is now a full-time
writer of children's geography and science books.

Picture Credits

Pages: 1: PhotoDisc Inc./Glen Allison. 3: PhotoDisc
Inc./Santokh Kochar. 4: Hutchison Photo
Library/David Culverd. 7: PhotoDisc Inc./Santokh
Kochar. 8: Hutchison Photo Library/Jeremy Horner.
9: Hutchison Photo Library/Juliet Highet.10: PhotoDisc
Inc./Santokh Kochar. 10-11: Hutchison Photo Library.
12 top: Hutchison Photo Library/Jeremy Horner.
12-13 bottom: Hutchison Photo Library/Nigara Film
Workshop. 15 and 16: Hutchison Photo Library/Jeremy
Horner. 18: Hutchison Photo Library/Liba Taylor.
19: Hutchison Photo Library/Nancy Durrell McKenna.
20: Eye Ubiquitous/David Cumming. 21: Yann Arthus-
Bertrand/CORBIS Pictures. 22 top: Hutchison Photo
Library/M. Jelliffe. 22 bottom: Hutchison Photo Library.
24: Hutchison Photo Library/Maurice Harvey.
25: Hutchison Photo Library. 26 top: Hutchison Photo
Library/Jeremy Horner. 26 bottom: James Davis Travel
Photography/James Davis. 28-29: PhotoDisc Inc./Ingo
Jezierski. 30: PhotoDisc Inc./Santokh Kochar.
31: PhotoDisc Inc./Ingo Jezierski.
Cover photo: Eye Ubiquitous Photo Library.

The Author

Lizann Flatt is an award-winning author and editor of children's non-fiction books and magazines.

Note to parents and teachers

Contents

Welcome to India

The Republic of India is the largest country in South Asia. Its people call it Bharat. India has the second-largest population in the world.

A rich and varied land

India has a long history. There are many temples and holy sites in India. The country is known for its textiles, tea, and diamonds. India has large cities and many small villages. Poor people live next to rich people.

Regions and Neighbors

India is made up of 28 states and 7 territories, including the Andaman, Nicobar, and Lakshadweep islands. Its northern neighbors are Pakistan, Nepal, Bhutan, Bangladesh, China, and Myanmar.

Below. **Dal Lake in Kashmir in northern India. The boats are lined up waiting for tourists to rent them.**

35°N
70°E
AFGHANISTAN

75°E

80°E
Leh

C H I N A

85°E   90°E   95°E

PAKISTAN

Indus

30°N

Amritsar

NEPAL

BHUTAN

Brahmaputra

25°N

New Delhi

Jaipur

Agra

Lucknow

INDO-GANGETIC PLAIN

Yamuna

Varanasi

Ganga (Ganges)

BANGLADESH

Tropic of Cancer

**G R E A T
I N D I A N
D E S E R T**

MYANMAR

Indus

Ahmedabad

**VINDHYA
MOUNTAINS**

Narmada

Surat

I N D I A

Nagpur

Calcutta

20°N

**DECCAN
PLATEAU**

Mumbai

Godavari

**ARABIAN
SEA**

**BAY OF
BENGAL**

Hyderabad

EASTERN GHATS

Krishna

WESTERN GHATS

N
W   E
S

Goa

15°N

Penner

Bangalore

Chennai

Mysore

**Lakshadweep
(Laccadive)
Islands**

Pondicherry

**Andaman
Islands**

	Desert
	Mountains
	Grassland and farming
□ Capital	○ Major city
——	Country boundary
- - -	Disputed boundary

10°N

Madurai

Thiruvananthapuram

0 ——————— 500 Miles

0 ——————— 750 Kilometers

Nicobar Islands

INDIAN OCEAN

**SRI
LANKA**

5

The Land

India is made up of three areas—the Himalaya mountains, the Indo-Gangetic Plain, and the Peninsula.

The Himalayas

The Himalaya mountains are covered with snow, but tropical plants, rice, and fruit trees grow in the valleys.

The Indo-Gangetic Plain

This area is mainly farmland and it is where most people live. Three great rivers flow across the plain—the Indus, Ganga, and Brahmaputra rivers.

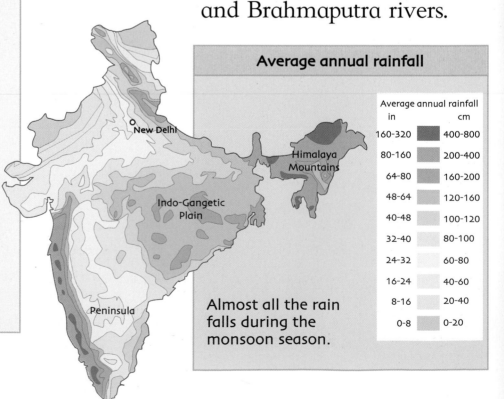

Average annual rainfall

| Average annual rainfall | |
in	cm
160-320	400-800
80-160	200-400
64-80	160-200
48-64	120-160
40-48	100-120
32-40	80-100
24-32	60-80
16-24	40-60
8-16	20-40
0-8	0-20

Almost all the rain falls during the monsoon season.

Above. **The city of Pushkar in Rajasthan, northwestern India. The city is on the edge of the Great Indian Desert. This desert is the driest part of India and is on the Indo-Gangetic Plain.**

Below. **Highest and lowest temperatures for Calcutta and Amritsar.**

The Peninsula

The Peninsula stretches to the southern tip of India. The Western Ghats and the Eastern Ghats run on each side of the coast. There are many forests on the Peninsula.

Climate

India has three seasons: winter (November to March), summer (April to June), and the monsoon (July to October). During the monsoon it rains every day in most places.

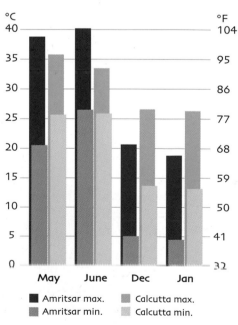

	Amritsar max.	Calcutta max.
	Amritsar min.	Calcutta min.

The People

Just over 1 billion people live in India. Only China has more people. India's culture is more than 4,500 years old.

■ Female   ■ Male

48%   52%

Above. **India has more men than women.**

Below. **Women wash themselves and their clothes in a river. India's great rivers play an important part in religion and in everyday life.**

Multicultural

Over its long history, many different peoples have settled in or invaded India. Most of them came overland from the northeast and northwest. Each of them added to the culture and languages of India. They helped to make the mixed and different peoples of India today.

Many languages

Hindi is the national language of India, but there are 18 official languages. Most people know at least one official language. English is the main language used by businesses and the government.

Two of Asia's oldest cultures come from India. The Indus Valley civilization was successful in the north for nearly 1,000 years. When the Aryans invaded in around 1500 B.C.E., it is thought that people from the Indus Valley were pushed out. They formed the Dravidian civilization in central and southern India.

Left. People at a street market in Orissa state, east India. The market is outside a Hindu temple.

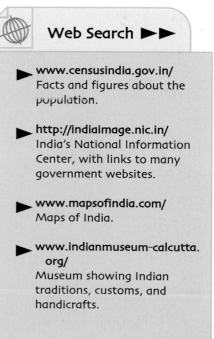

Web Search ►►

► www.censusindia.gov.in/
Facts and figures about the population.

► http://indiaimage.nic.in/
India's National Information Center, with links to many government websites.

► www.mapsofindia.com/
Maps of India.

► www.indianmuseum-calcutta.org/
Museum showing Indian traditions, customs, and handicrafts.

Town and Country Life

Most Indians live in villages and small towns in the countryside. However, many young people are moving to the cities to find work and a better life.

City houses with servants

Cities are overcrowded but the houses have piped water and electricity. Rich families have large houses and several servants. Middle-class families live in apartments or small houses.

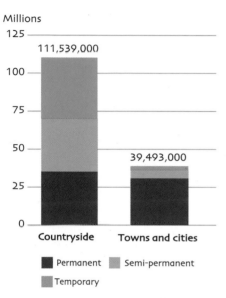

Millions

111,539,000

39,493,000

Countryside   Towns and cities

■ Permanent   ■ Semi-permanent
■ Temporary

Above. **The number of different kinds of homes in cities and villages.**

Below. **In the countryside, most people work on the land. They often use animals instead of machines.**

Villages

In the villages, rich families may have two-story brick houses with electricity and piped water. Poor families have houses made from mud and straw or wood and palm leaves. Not all villages have electricity, and many houses have no piped water. Instead, people pump drinking water from wells and carry it to their homes. They bathe and wash their clothes in nearby lakes or streams.

Above. **City homes with piped drinking water.**

Above. **Village homes with piped drinking water.**

Below. **In big cities such as Mumbai, many poor people live in slums. They make shelters using cardboard and sheets of iron.**

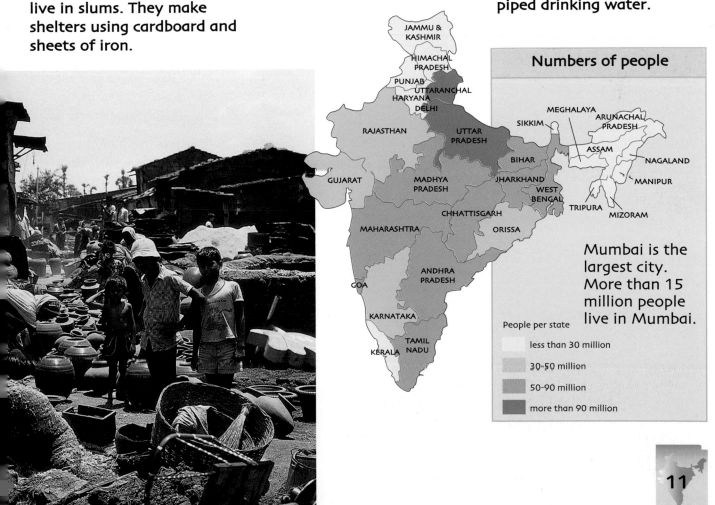

Mumbai is the largest city. More than 15 million people live in Mumbai.

Numbers of people

People per state

less than 30 million

30-50 million

50-90 million

more than 90 million

JAMMU & KASHMIR
HIMACHAL PRADESH
PUNJAB
UTTARANCHAL
HARYANA
DELHI
RAJASTHAN
UTTAR PRADESH
GUJARAT
MADHYA PRADESH
JHARKHAND
BIHAR
SIKKIM
MEGHALAYA
ARUNACHAL PRADESH
ASSAM
NAGALAND
MANIPUR
WEST BENGAL
TRIPURA
MIZORAM
CHHATTISGARH
ORISSA
MAHARASHTRA
GOA
ANDHRA PRADESH
KARNATAKA
KERALA
TAMIL NADU

Above. Tea leaves are picked by hand on tea plantations in Darjeeling, northern India.

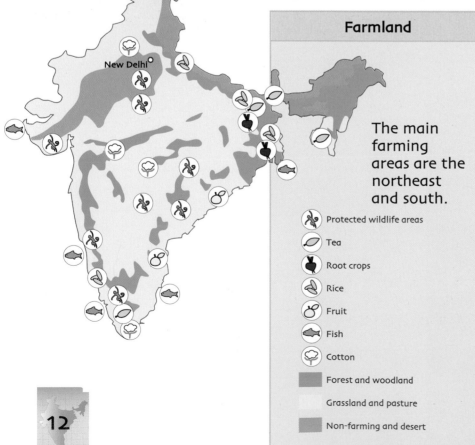

New Delhi

Farmland

The main farming areas are the northeast and south.

- Protected wildlife areas
- Tea
- Root crops
- Rice
- Fruit
- Fish
- Cotton
- Forest and woodland
- Grassland and pasture
- Non-farming and desert

Farming and Fishing

More than half the people in India work in farming. India produces a lot of milk, sugar, fruit, and grain. Fishing is important along the coast.

Farming and food

Farmers grow rice and wheat all year round. They also grow vegetables, spices, and fruits. Factories produce cookies, chocolate, pasta, and soft drinks.

Fishing

India's fishermen catch the sixth-largest amount of fish in the world. Most of the fish are frozen or canned and then sold to other countries. Some fish are made into food for chickens.

Production each year

Milk   74,700,000 tons
Fish   5,260,000 tons
Meat   4,500,000 tons
Sugarcane   295,700,000 tons
Bread   1,500,000 tons
Biscuits 1,100,000 tons
Cocoa products such as chocolate 34,000 tons

Eggs   30,150,000,000

Cotton   12,200,000 bales
Jute & hemp
        9,700,000 bales
Soft drinks
    6,320,000,000 bottles

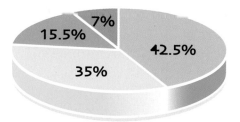

7%
15.5%
42.5%
35%

Wheat 70.78 million tonnes/tons
Other cereals 31.4 million tonnes/tons
Peas, beans, legumes 14.8 million tonnes/tons
Rice 86 million tonnes/tons

Above. **Amount of each crop produced in India.**

Left. **Local fishermen bring in their catch on a beach in the state of Kerala.**

Resources and Industry

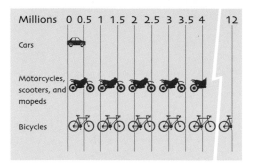

Above. **Number of road vehicles made each year.**

India is rich in many minerals. It uses these and other resources to make things. India is one of the largest industrial countries in the world.

Resources

India's largest resource is coal. It has enough coal to last 100 years. India is also the world's largest producer of mica, which is used in industry. Other major resources include iron ore, bauxite, lignite, crude oil, natural gas, and diamonds.

Energy

India produces lots of energy. All cities and most villages are now supplied with electricity. Most power is made from coal, but India also has hydroelectric and nuclear power plants. However, the amount of electricity needed is greater than the amount made, so power blackouts are common. Some villagers still have to collect wood from forests, and burn waste and cow dung as fuels.

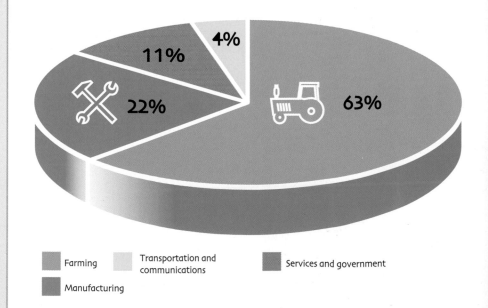

Farming
Manufacturing
Transportation and communications
Services and government

Above. **Percentages of workers in major industries.**

14

Industries

About 20 million people work in India's textile industry. They make thread, cloth, clothes, and carpets. Other important industries include leather, steel, cars, food, electronics, and computer software.

Above. Trees in Tamil Nadu in southern India are cut down and used for timber.

Below. Weight of industrial products made each year.

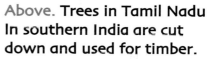

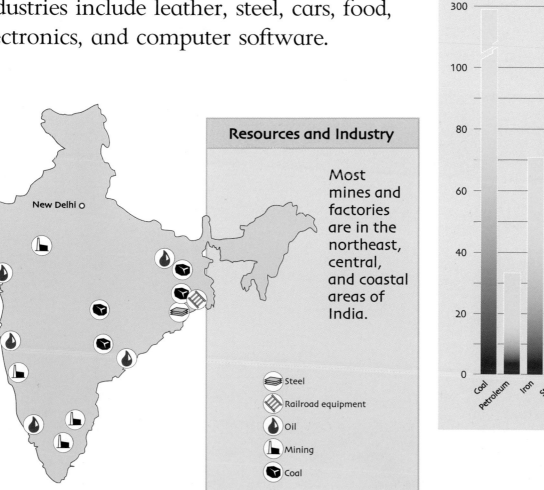

Resources and Industry

Most mines and factories are in the northeast, central, and coastal areas of India.

New Delhi o

Steel
Railroad equipment
Oil
Mining
Coal

Millions of tonnes/tons

300
100
80
60
40
20
0

Coal Petroleum Iron Steel Aluminum Fertilizers Jute

Transportation

Most people use buses and trains to travel across India. A growing number of people travel by car. Air travel is also becoming more popular.

Roads

India has more than 1,864,000 miles (3,000,000km) of roads. Many are narrow and crowded, so the government is intending to build new main roads and highways.

Railway Network

India has the second-largest rail network in the world. Every day, trains carry 12 million people and more than a million tons of freight. High-speed trains connect New Delhi with other major cities.

Below. **Railroad workers repair tracks at Jaisalmer in Rajasthan.**

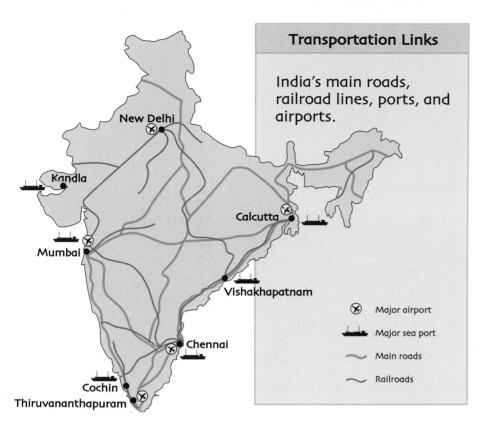

Transportation Links

India's main roads, railroad lines, ports, and airports.

New Delhi ✕
Kandla ⚓
Calcutta ✕
Mumbai ✕
Vishakhapatnam ⚓
Chennai ✕
Cochin ⚓
Thiruvananthapuram ✕

✕ Major airport
⚓ Major sea port
〰 Main roads
〰 Railroads

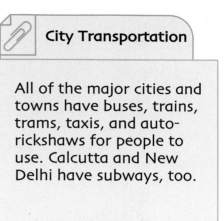

City Transportation

All of the major cities and towns have buses, trains, trams, taxis, and auto-rickshaws for people to use. Calcutta and New Delhi have subways, too.

Below. Motor vehicles bought in India.

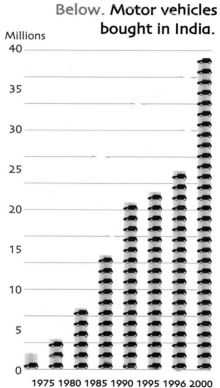

Millions
40
35
30
25
20
15
10
5
0

1975 1980 1985 1990 1995 1996 2000

Ships

India has many huge oil tankers and cargo ships. Hundreds of smaller ships work along the coast. In the states of Kerala and West Bengal, barges, ships, and ferries carry people and goods up and down the rivers.

Air travel

India has about 350 airports. Several airplanes fly each day between the major cities. New Delhi and Mumbai are the main international airports, with flights to other Asian countries and Europe.

Web Search ▶▶

▶ www.mapsofindia.com/distances
Distances and routes between most cities and major towns.

▶ www.indianrail.gov.in
India's railroad system.

▶ www.airindia.com
India's major airlines.

Education

Education in India is getting better. In 1951 only 18 percent of the people could read. By 2000, 58 percent could read.

Schools

The government provides free schooling for all children between the ages of six and 14. Even so, some families are so poor the children have to work instead of going to school. The school day lasts from 9 A.M. to 3:30 P.M. After the age of 14, many children go to secondary school. Children study languages, math, science, geography, history, and physical education.

Below. **Pupils at primary school (aged 6 to 10 years).**

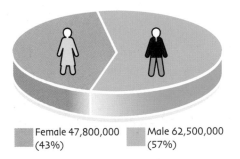

Female 47,800,000 (43%) Male 62,500,000 (57%)

Below. **Pupils at middle school (aged 11 to 14 years).**

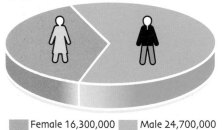

Female 16,300,000 (39.7%) Male 24,700,000 (60.3%)

Below. **Pupils at secondary school (aged 14+ years).**

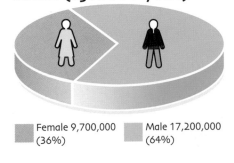

Female 9,700,000 (36%) Male 17,200,000 (64%)

Below. **Women learning to read and write at a class for adults. The government is helping many adults learn new skills so everyone is better educated.**

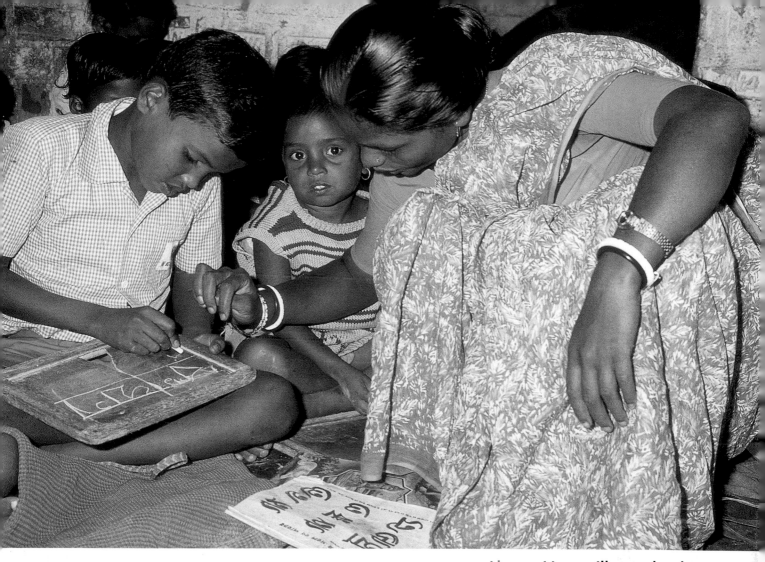

Above. **Many village schools use slate boards and chalk for writing instead of paper and pens.**

Children in cities often go to private schools, for which their parents must pay. After secondary school, pupils can go to university. Many students study at universities abroad.

Left. **The number of men and women who go to university in India.**

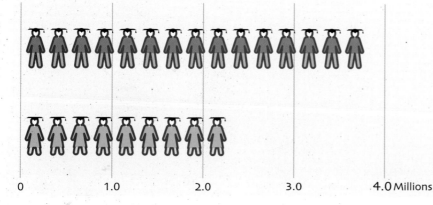

Web Search ▶▶

▶ www.goidirectory.nic.in/ Government information on education.

Sport and Leisure

Indians play many different sports. Hockey and cricket are the most popular.

Hockey

Hockey is India's national sport. The national hockey team has won eight gold medals at the Olympic Games.

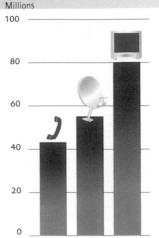

Above. **Households with telephone lines, satellite connections, and TVs.**

Below. **Several games of cricket are being played in this park in Calcutta.**

Other sports

Children play cricket in parks and on the streets. Everyone follows important matches on TV or radio. Other sports include tennis, chess, archery, and judo. Elephant racing and camel racing are also popular.

Leisure activities

Rich people in India like to go to the theater and the movies. Poorer people who cannot afford this watch television instead. Often, people who do not own a TV go to the house of someone who does.

Left. Polo is played on horseback with a ball and long sticks. The game is also played in Britain and other countries.

Web Search ▶▶

▶ www.air.kode.net/
All India Radio (AIR).

▶ http://timesofindia.indiatimes.com/articlelist/671208.cms
Times of India sports news.

▶ www.tourisminindia.com/
Sports events and leisure attractions.

Above. A Hindu holy man and a tourist ride on an elephant through the streets of Udaipur, Rajasthan.

Right. Hindu holy men meditate beside the Ganga River at Varanasi.

Daily Life and Religion

Most Indian people's life is centered around religion. The main religions in India are Hinduism, Islam, Buddhism, and Sikhism.

Religion

There are temples, holy sites, and religious statues all over India. Hindus worship in their homes as well as in temples. Many homes have a shrine to one of the Hindu gods. Muslims are followers of Islam. They pray five times each day and may go to their mosque on Fridays. The most holy Sikh temple is in Amritsar in the north-west. Buddhists worship in temples and make offerings at shrines and monasteries.

Shopping

Bazaars, or local markets, are everywhere. The stands sell almost everything, from food and clothes to candy and toys. In private shops, people bargain for the price of what they buy. But government shops in the cities sell goods at fixed prices. The largest cities also have shopping malls.

Below. How families spend their money each year.

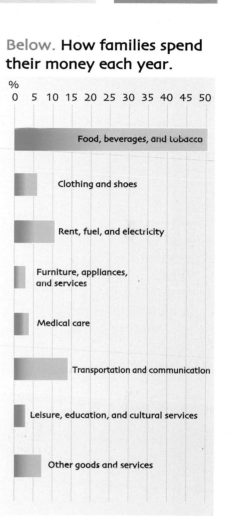

%

0 5 10 15 20 25 30 35 40 45 50

Food, beverages, and tobacco

Clothing and shoes

Rent, fuel, and electricity

Furniture, appliances, and services

Medical care

Transportation and communication

Leisure, education, and cultural services

Other goods and services

Web Search ►►

► http://indiaimage.nic.in/
India's National Information Centre.

► www.indiaserver.com/
Official news stories.

Arts and Media

Indian movies are world famous. Music, theater, television, radio, and other forms of art are also important.

Radio, television, and newspapers

All India Radio (AIR) has 198 radio stations, and 90 percent of people watch national television. Many Indians also watch satellite and cable TV. Most newspapers are published in Hindi.

Below. A concert hall in Chennai, a temple city in Tamil Nadu.

Tourists

India has become a popular place to visit. More than 2 million tourists travel to India each year. They go to see ancient temples, colorful fairs, and golden beaches.

Bollywood

More movies are made in India (over 900 every year) than in Hollywood. Watching moves is very popular and movie theaters are everywhere.

The city of Mumbai is nicknamed "Bollywood" because it is the center of the Indian movie industry.

Above. An advertisement for a "Bollywood" movie.

Web Search ►►

► www.webindia.com/
Indian music, crafts, and dance.

► www.ddindia.com/
Doordarshan Indian TV station.

► www.timesofindia.com/
Times of India newspaper.

► www.hinduonline.com/
The Hindu newspaper site.

Government

The modern Republic of India was founded in 1947. The leaders of the country are the president, the vice president, and the prime minister.

The president

The president is the head of state and commander-in-chief of the armed forces. He or she works with a council of ministers and advisors.

Above. India Gate is a World War I memorial. It is in New Delhi, the capital city of India.

Below. Government House in Bangalore, the capital city of the state of Karnataka.

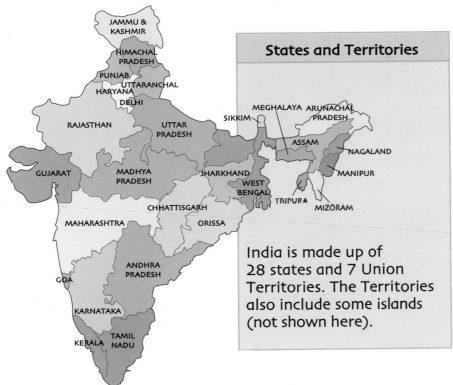

States and Territories

India is made up of 28 states and 7 Union Territories. The Territories also include some islands (not shown here).

Below. **How the Indian government spends money each year.**

Percentage of total money spent

(bar chart categories: Interest and debt, Transportation, State grants, Defense, Communications, Farming, Social services)

Elections

All Indian citizens can vote from the age of 18. They elect members to represent them in the Lok Sabha (House of the People). The prime minister is the leader of the political party that wins the most votes in a national election. The prime minister and the council of ministers run the country.

State government

Each state has its own governors who are elected by the ordinary people. These governors elect people to sit in the national Council of States.

Web Search ▶▶

▶ www.indiabudget.nic.in/
How the government spends its money

▶ www.goidirectory.nic.in/
Directory of government websites.

▶ www.pib.nic.in/
India's Press Information Bureau.

Place in the World

India's civilizations are thousands of years old, but the modern Republic of India is still quite young.

Making progress

The Indian government aims to make the electricity and transportation systems better. It also wants more people to be educated.

International links

India is part of such international organizations as the United Nations, the World Health Organization, and Interpol, an international police group. India is also a member of organizations that encourage countries in Asia to work together. These organizations try to help the poor and stop fighting at the borders. India has recently increased its trade with the rest of the world. This has made the country richer.

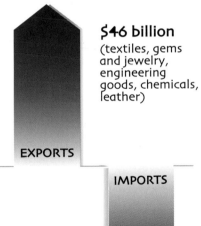

$46 billion
(textiles, gems and jewelry, engineering goods, chemicals, leather)

EXPORTS

IMPORTS

$56 billion
(crude oil and petroleum products, machinery, gems, fertilizer, chemicals)

Above. **India's imports and exports.**

Left. **The Taj Mahal in Agra. It is the tomb of an Indian empress who died in 1631.**

Area:
1,269,220 sq miles
(3,287,263 sq km)

Population size:
846,300,000 (1991
Census); 1,000,100,000
(2000 estimate)

Capital city:
New Delhi

Other major cities:
Mumbai, Calcutta, Chennai,
Bangalore, Hyderabad

Longest Rivers:
Brahmaputra (1,832 miles/
2,948km), Indus (1,976
miles/ 3,180km),
Ganga (1,560 miles/
2,510km)

Highest mountain:
Kanchenjunga
(28,208ft/8,598m)

Currency:
Indian rupees (Rs)
1 rupee = 100 paise

Flag:
Orange, white, and green

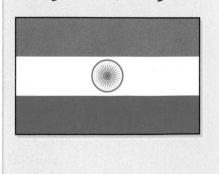

horizontal bands. The white
band has a blue wheel in it.

Languages:
18 official languages
including Hindi, Bengali,
Urdu, Gujarati, Punjabi.
English commonly used and
understood.

Major resources:
coal, mica, iron ore,
bauxite, lignite, aluminum,
chromite, manganese,
titanium, crude oil, natural
gas, diamonds, and
limestone.

Major exports:
textiles, gems and jewelry,
machinery, chemicals,
leather, marine products,
rice, tea.

**National holidays and
major events:**
January 26: Republic Day
May 1: May Day/Labor Day
August 15: Independence
  Day
October 2: Mahatma
  Gandhi's Birthday
December 25: Christmas
  Day

Religions:
Religions followed include
Hinduism, Islam,
Buddhism, Jainism,
Sikhism, Christianity,
Zoroastrianism, Judaism

Key Words

AUTO-RICKSHAWS
Small passenger vehicles powered by motor scooters.

CIVILIZATION
A group of people with its own culture, art, way of life, and government.

CLIMATE
The type of weather a place usually has at different times of the year.

CULTURE
A group of people following the same traditions for many generations.

EMPIRE
A group of countries or lands ruled by a single country.

EXPORTS
Goods sold to a foreign country.

GOVERNMENT
The group of people that runs a country, making new laws, raising taxes, and organizing health, education, transportation, and other national systems.

HYDROELECTRIC POWER
Electrical power generated from flowing water.

IMPORTS
Goods bought from a foreign country.

INDUSTRY
Mines, factories, and businesses that make money.

JUTE
A plant used to make mats, sacks, and string.

MINERAL
The form in which metals and other resources occur in rocks and in the soil.

MONSOON
Wind that blows from the sea and brings heavy rainy.

REPUBLIC
A country whose head of state is elected to govern.

PLANTATIONS
Areas of farmland where trees and shrubs are grown for their fruit and leaves.

RESOURCES
A country's supplies of energy, natural materials, and minerals.

SLUMS
Areas of dirty, overcrowded houses and unpaved streets.

STATE
Part of a country that has its own government but is part of the national government.

TERRITORIES
Areas of land governed by a country.

TROPICAL
The part of the Earth that lies between the Tropic of Cancer and the Tropic of Capricorn: "tropical" can also mean the hot and damp weather of that region.

Index